# VERSES OF LIFE

POETRY

RAYEES ALI

Made with ♥ on the Notion Press Platform
www.notionpress.com

Title: Verses of Life

Verses of Life" is a poetry collection that explores the complexities of the human experience. The poems in this collection touch on themes such as love, loss, joy, struggle, and growth. Through vivid imagery and powerful language, the author invites readers to reflect on their own experiences and emotions, and find inspiration and wisdom in the journey of life. Each verse offers a unique perspective on the human condition, making "Verses of Life" a moving and insightful read for anyone looking to explore the depths of the human heart and soul.

Top of Form

Author's Note:

Writing "Verses of Life" has been a labor of love for me. This collection of poems represents my experiences, thoughts, and emotions over the course of my life. Each verse tells a story and reflects a moment in time that has had a profound impact on me.

I hope that these verses will resonate with readers and inspire them to reflect on their own experiences, find solace in their struggles, and celebrate their triumphs. Life is a journey, and I believe that the power of poetry lies in its ability to capture the essence of that journey, to distill our experiences into a few lines that can touch the hearts of others.

I am grateful for the opportunity to share my words with the world and for the support of those who have encouraged me along the way. I dedicate this book to anyone who has ever felt lost, alone, or uncertain on their path through life. May these verses offer you comfort, wisdom, and inspiration as you navigate the twists and turns of your own journey.

Top of Form

## Introduction:

Verses of Life is a collection of poems that explore different aspects of life, nature, and society. Each poem takes the reader on a journey through the beauty and complexity of our world, inviting us to reflect on the deeper meanings that lie beneath the surface. From the tranquility of a snowy winter to the frenzy of the stock market, from the mysteries of history to the simplicity of a cycle ride, these poems capture the essence of what it means to be alive.

Chapter 1: Winter's Charm This chapter includes poems that celebrate the magic of winter, with its snowflakes, frost, and chilly cold. The poems explore the charm of the winter season, as well as the feelings of love and nostalgia that it can evoke.

Chapter 2: Life Before Internet In this chapter, the poems reflect on life before the age of the internet and social media. They highlight the joys of living in a small circle of reality, where honesty, nature, and face-to-face communication were the norm.

Chapter 3: My Book This chapter celebrates the power of books and the knowledge they contain. The poems delve into different subjects, from economics and politics to science and mathematics, showing how books can open up new worlds of understanding.

Chapter 4: The Virtual World The poems in this chapter explore the duality between reality and virtuality, and the way we experience and express our feelings in the online world.

Chapter 5: Cycle of Life This chapter focuses on the cycle of life, with poems that depict the running, riding, and flowing of life, as well as the changing seasons and the beauty of nature.

Chapter 6: Finance and Accounts These poems explore the world of finance and accounting, highlighting the importance of money and degrees in our society.

Chapter 7: The Stock Market This chapter delves into the frenzy of the stock market, with its ups and downs, and the emotions and feelings that arise when investing in stocks.

Chapter 8: Winter in Kashmir The poems in this chapter capture the freezing and nasty cold of winter in Kashmir, as well as the beauty of the snow and the apathy of the landscape.

Chapter 9: Saffron Fields This chapter celebrates the saffron fields of Kashmir, with their delicate petals and corms, as well as the trees and populars that surround them.

Chapter 10: Career The poems in this chapter explore the beginning and end of careers, and the role that money and love can play in our professional lives.

Chapter 11: History This chapter takes us on a journey through the pages of history, highlighting the social customs, freedom, and blazing that have shaped our world.

Chapter 12: Clouds and Sky These poems depict the endless skies and the beauty of clouds, snowflakes, and water, evoking a sense of wonder and awe.

Chapter 13: Frozen River In this chapter, the poems explore the image of a frozen river, as a symbol of death, imagination, and apathy.

Conclusion: Verses of Life is a celebration of the beauty and complexity of our world, as seen through the eyes of poetry. The poems in this collection offer a glimpse into the many facets of life, from the winter's charm to the saffron fields of Kashmir, from the stock market to the pages of history.

## FIRST DAY AT SCHOOL

A new day dawns, so bright and clear
A journey begins, without any fear
Off to school, a world so new
A place of beauty, where dreams come true

The Chinar trees stand tall and proud
Their leaves rustling, a soothing sound

The school bell rings, a wake-up call
A day of adventure, for one and all

Gulzar, the peon, greets with a smile
A helping hand, to guide for a while
Through the halls, so grand and wide
Excitement fills, from deep inside

The first lesson, a world to explore
A world of wonder, that we adore
But wait, what's this? A lunch break's near
Time to relax, without any fear

Making new friends, so warm and kind
Together they eat, sharing what they find
The day goes by, too fast it seems
But memories made, will last like dreams

The first day of school, a day to remember
A day so special, that we'll always treasure
A world of beauty, that we've just found
A place to learn, and forever be bound.

## WINTER`S INN

Winter's chilly breath is here to stay
As snowflakes dance and frost takes hold

**The trees stand bare, their leaves away**
**A sight to see, so pure and cold**

**Khrebal mountains rise so high**
**And catch the snow upon their peaks**
**As winter winds go rushing by**
**A symphony of sound it speaks**

**The lanes are lined with snowdrifts deep**
**And crunch beneath your every step**
**As winter's magic takes its keep**
**A frozen world, where memories kept**

**The karewas lay covered in white**
**A winter wonderland so still**
**A peaceful sight, a calming sight**
**A frozen land with winter's chill**

**Winter, oh winter, you're so grand**
**A season of beauty, so pristine**
**You paint a picture, with your icy hand**
**A world of wonder, a true dream.**

**In the small village of Rasool Kak**
**Didi's kitchen was never slack**
**With Sullu Kak and his big appetite**
**A new invention, they did ignite**

## THE BREAD MAKER

The bread maker, a wonderous device
A tandoor in disguise, oh so nice
No more kneading, no more fuss
Just add the dough and let it suss

The aroma of bread filled the air
As Didi's bread maker worked with care
No more waiting for the dough to rise
Or worrying about the perfect size

The kulche cooked to perfection
A symphony of taste and confection
The bread maker had done its job
Leaving everyone's taste buds to throb

Now, every day is a joyous feast
With Didi's bread maker at the very least
Sullu Kak's appetite was never sated
But the bread maker had them all elated.

A new day dawns, so bright and clear
A journey begins, without any fear
Off to school, a world so new
A place of beauty, where dreams come true

## The chinar tree

The Chinar trees stand tall and proud
Their leaves rustling, a soothing sound
The school bell rings, a wake-up call
A day of adventure, for one and all

Gulzar, the peon, greets with a smile
A helping hand, to guide for a while
Through the halls, so grand and wide
Excitement fills, from deep inside

The first lesson, a world to explore
A world of wonder, that we adore
But wait, what's this? A lunch break's near
Time to relax, without any fear

Making new friends, so warm and kind
Together they eat, sharing what they find
The day goes by, too fast it seems
But memories made, will last like dreams

The first day of school, a day to remember
A day so special, that we'll always treasure
A world of beauty, that we've just found
A place to learn, and forever be bound.

## RADIO

Radio, oh radio, the sound of the air
A voice so clear, for all to hear
A world of music, at your command
A world so vast, across the land

Mothers listen to lullabies
As children dream, with sleepy eyes
Old men tune in, to relive the past
A world of memories, that always last

The beggar on the street, with nothing to give
Finds solace in music, as long as he lives
The radio fills, his heart and soul
A world of sound, to make him whole

A voice in the darkness, a ray of light
The radio brings, the world so bright
A symphony of sound, that echoes within
A world of music, to help you win

So tune in, and listen close
A world of music, at your dispose
Let the radio, take you away
To a world of wonder, and a brighter day.

## MOBILE A WONDER

Mobile, oh mobile, so swift and light
A world of wonder, that's always in sight
YouTube videos, for learning and fun
A world of jobs, that's just begun

Music in your pocket, wherever you go
A symphony of sound, that fills your soul
Vlogging, for all the world to see
A world of wonder, that's truly free

In touch with friends, no matter the distance
A world of connection, without any resistance
Social media, to share and trade
A world of commerce, where deals are made

Mobile, oh mobile, you're always near
A world of wonder, that's always clear
So take it with you, wherever you roam
A world of magic, that's truly your own.

## THE DARK NIGHT AND BELOVED

In the darkness of the night,
My beloved's face shines bright.
Waiting for her, my heart beats fast

Longing for her, to end this vast

The moon above, a guiding light
Shining down, with all its might
My love for her, like a pinnacle
A tower of strength, that's unbreakable

The night so still, so calm and serene
A world of wonder, that's just a dream
But in her arms, I find my home
A world of love, that's forever flown

The night and my lover, a perfect pair
A world of love, without any care
In her embrace, I find my peace
A world of love, that'll never cease

So let the night be dark and deep
In my beloved's arms, I'll forever sleep
For in her love, I find my light
A world of wonder, that's always right.

## THE CHINAR TREE

Amidst the chinar's towering height,

A sparrow sings a tune so bright,

Her melody fills the tranquil air,

As she flits from branch to branch with flair.

The sky above is a vibrant blue,

A perfect backdrop for this view,

Ducks glide by on a nearby stream,

As the sparrow chases a fleeting dream.

Weeds and greenery adorn the ground,

Vegetation all around abounds,

And the tree sways with every breeze,

Its shakeness a sight to please.

A pomegranate hangs ripe and red,

As snowflakes dance upon its head,

A cozy nest in the tree's embrace,

Is the sparrow's peaceful resting place.

COMPUTER:

**A marvel of modern innovation,**

**A machine that sparked a revolution,**

**The computer, a tool of creation,**

**An invention that deserves celebration.**

**It's a gateway to endless knowledge,**

**A means to hone our skills in college,**

**A place to watch videos and shows,**

**To learn new things and see how it goes.**

**With access to books at our fingertips,**

**We can delve into any subject and grips,**

**And explore the world's vast diversity,**

**From science to arts and all that's worthy.**

**A wonder of numeric precision,**

**It solves math problems with ease and vision,**

**With algorithms that make calculations,**

A tool that eases our computations.

In the office, it's a vital aid,

To manage tasks and plans that are made,

With software that makes work less tiring,

And keeps us organized and inspiring.

The computer, a tool that we depend on,

A machine that keeps us moving on,

A creation that's forever evolving,

A marvel that's always problem-solving.

The roads we travel,

both near and far,

## ROADS TO HEAVEN

A lifeline that connects us where we are,

A web of pathways that spans the land,

A means to reach out and take a stand.

**With skills of driving, we navigate,**

**Through twists and turns, and heavy weight,**

**A journey that can be full of wonder,**

**With sights and sounds that pull us under.**

**The hum of motors, a steady drone,**

**The wheels that carry us to our home,**

**With every mile that passes by,**

**The road reveals more than meets the eye.**

**Feelings of excitement,**

**hope, and fear,**

**As we set out on the journey here,**

**The road ahead an unknown fate,**

**A path that leads to our own gate.**

**The pavement stretches far and wide,**

**A path to follow with no need to hide,**

The road a mirror of our own life,

With twists and turns, joy and strife.

The roads we travel shape our souls,

A journey that makes us whole,

A lifeline that connects us all,

A means to rise up and stand tall.

So let us take the road less traveled,

And discover what lies unraveled,

For in the journey we find our way,

And make our mark, day by day.

Pomegranate tree and my house

In the yard of my childhood home,

Stood a pomegranate tree all alone,

With leaves of green and fruits of red,

A symbol of life that never shed.

**As a child, I watched it grow,**

**With roots so deep, it seemed to know,**

**The secrets of the earth beneath,**

**And the seasons that bring its leaf.**

**In my youth,**

**I played under its shade,**

**With friends and family,**

**we laughed and played,**

**And the tree stood tall,**

**a silent witness,**

**To our joys and sorrows,**

**both bleak and bliss.**

**In winter, the snow would fall,**

**And the tree would wear a white shawl,**

**But still, it stood with a steadfast grace,**

A beauty that no season could erase.

In spring,

the water dripped from its leaves,

A melody that the heart perceives,

A soothing sound that calms the mind,

And brings a peace that's hard to find.

And now, as I look back in time,

I see the tree,

still standing in its prime,

A symbol of my childhood home,

And the memories that will never roam.

For every leaf,

every fruit,

every sound,

Is a part of me that will always be found,

**In the pomegranate tree of my youth,**

**A symbol of life, love, and truth.**

**Winter's Beauty.**

**Amidst the winter's icy reign,**

**A world of white and stillness plain.**

**Snowflakes falling from the sky,**

**A wonderland for the naked eye.**

**The parakeets have flown away,**

**To warmer climes they cannot stay.**

**But in their place, the birds of gray,**

**Now forage in the snow each day.**

**The frost has painted on the trees,**

**A masterpiece for all to see.**

**But lifeless branches, once alive,**

**Are now a stark and chilling sight.**

And yet, imagination thrives,

In winter's grasp, it comes alive.

For in the snow, a canvas grand,

A world of art at our command.

Death may seem to be at hand,

As nature sheds its vibrant band.

But life still stirs beneath the ground,

Waiting for the spring to come around.

So let us marvel at the snow,

And all its magic, let it show.

For in this winter wonderland,

A beauty that will always stand.

## LIFE BEFORE INTERNET

Life before the internet,

Was a simpler time,

**no need to fret.**

**A small circle of friends we'd keep,**

**And in reality,**

**our bonds would deepen.**

**No virtuality to escape to,**

**Our lives were filled with charm and hue.**

**Honesty was the norm back then,**

**A virtue we held dear, even then.**

**Nature was our playground and muse,**

**Its beauty and wonder, ours to choose.**

**We'd spend our days outside in the sun,**

**Playing games and having fun.**

**We'd read books and write letters by hand,**

**Connect with loved ones across the land.**

**We'd go on adventures and explore,**

Without a screen to distract us anymore.

Life before the internet,

Was a time we'll never forget.

For in its simplicity and grace,

We found a way to truly embrace.

The world around us, we held dear,

With no need for likes or followers near.

We were free to live and love,

And cherish the moments sent from above.

## MY BOOK

My book, my precious tome,

A gateway to the world beyond my home.

Its economy, society,

and politics I find,

In every page,

**a new world of the mind.**

**Science and maths,**

**statistics too,**

**Each chapter a journey,**

**a world anew.**

**The knowledge within,**

**a treasure trove,**

**Of secrets and wonders waiting to be strove.**

**From ancient times to modern days,**

**A wealth of wisdom in so many ways.**

**My book takes me on a journey grand,**

**To distant lands and far-off lands.**

**I learn of cultures and traditions rare,**

**Of people and places, beyond compare.**

**I explore the mysteries of the universe,**

The secrets of the atom, and the laws that it rehearse.

My book,

my trusty companion,

A friend in solitude,

a source of inspiration.

It opens doors to the unknown,

Expanding my horizons,

like seeds that are sown.

So here's to my book,

my beloved friend,

A portal to worlds without end.

May its pages continue to guide,

And broaden my knowledge far and wide.

## VIRTUAL WORLD

In this virtual world,

**we find,**

**A place to escape and unwind.**

**Reality fades into the night,**

**As we enter a world of virtual light.**

**Emotions take on a new sense,**

**As we connect through screens and vents.**

**Feelings expressed in text and chat,**

**A world of communication, just like that.**

**No boundaries or limits in this place,**

**As we explore new worlds with grace.**

**Our avatars roam without restraint,**

**A world of endless possibility,**

**without complaint.**

**But in this virtuality,**

**we must be aware, Of the line between truth and dare.**

For though the world we see is bright,

It cannot replace reality's light.

So let us enjoy this virtual ride,

And all the wonders that it provides.

But let us remember, deep inside,

That reality is where our true selves reside.

## MY CYCLE

My cycle, my trusty ride,

Through life's ups and downs,

we glide.

Running through fields and city streets,

Feeling the wind, beneath our feet.

Trees pass us by in a blur,

Their leaves rustling, like a purr.

We cycle on,

**enjoying the view,**

**Nature's beauty, a grand debut.**

**In the winter,**

**snowflakes fall,**

**Creating a wonderland,**

**a magic thrall.**

**We ride through the snow,**

**feeling free,**

**With the cold air,**

**a sense of glee.**

**In the rains,**

**we cycle with care,**

**The water splashing, like a dare.**

**But still, we push on with delight,**

**The raindrops falling, a wondrous sight.**

**Leaves fall in autumn's embrace,**

**Their colors a sight to embrace.**

**We cycle through them, with ease,**

**Feeling the joy of nature's breeze.**

**My cycle,**

**my faithful steed,**

**Through life's journey,**

**you take the lead.**

**We ride together,**

**through thick and thin,**

**My cycle,**

**my partner,**

**my friend within.**

## FINANACE

**In the world of finance and accounts,**

**We find the heartbeat of business amounts.**

**Accounting, a language all its own,**

**The backbone of any enterprise grown.**

**Numbers and figures,**

**balance sheets and more,**

**All in service of the business we adore.**

**Financial statements,**

**profit and loss,**

**A guide to success,**

**through any cost.**

**For in the world of business and life,**

**Money is a tool to reach new heights.**

**A means to an end,**

**a goal to achieve,**

**The foundation upon which we weave.**

So let us embrace the world of finance,

And all its challenges,

let us take a stance.

For in this realm,

lies the key,

To unlocking our true destiny.

Let us learn the language of accounts,

And navigate the world of finance with sound.

For in doing so,

we find the power,

To take our business and life to new flower.

## STOCK MARKET

In the world of stocks and the market,

A journey of discovery we embark it.

The stock market,

**a place of flux,**

**A playground of risk and trust.**

**Stocks rise and fall like the tide,**

**Investors watch with eyes open wide.**

**The SIPs and the BSE, NSE, and Nifty,**

**A world of options, some slow and some speedy.**

**Amazon, a behemoth of the trade,**

**Its stocks a wonder, a value to be made.**

**Investors rush to join the fray,**

**A chance to earn big, day by day.**

**But the market is not for the faint of heart,**

**A place where fortunes can quickly depart.**

**Risk and reward,**

**a balancing act,**

**A strategy,**

a game plan to enact.

For in the world of stocks and the market,

One must be wise, with judgment to target.

Patience, knowledge,

and strategy key,

To navigate the ups and downs with certainty.

So let us embrace the world of stocks,

And all the opportunities it unlocks.

With courage and care,

let us invest

And take on the market with our very best.

## WINTERS CHILL

In the heart of Kashmir, in winter's chill,

The air is crisp,

the cold a thrill.

**The Bageer,**

**frozen and still,**

**A world of wonder,**

**a sight to behold.**

**The hills and valleys,**

**draped in snow,**

**A beauty to behold,**

**a wondrous show.**

**The freezing air,**

**a biting embrace,**

**A reminder of winter's enduring grace.**

**The trees stand tall,**

**their branches bare,**

**A testament to nature's loving care.**

**Their leaves gone,**

but not their pride,

A sight to behold,

in winter's stride.

The sun, a distant,

hazy light,

But still,

the beauty of winter,

in sight.

The snow-covered landscape,

a winter's dream,

A world of magic,

or so it seems.

For in Kashmir's winter,

there is a glow,

A wonderland of snow,

**a magical tableau.**

**The chilly cold,**

**a reminder of life's flow,**

**A season of growth, a season of hope.**

## SAFFRON FIELDS

**In the fields of saffron,**

**a sight to see,**

**The trees,**

**the populars,**

**swaying in glee.**

**The corms,**

**like jewels,**

**tucked in the earth,**

**A promise of saffron's wondrous worth.**

**The petals,**

**delicate and pure,**

**A golden hue,**

**they do allure.**

**The fields alive with nature's sound,**

**A world of wonder, all around.**

**The saffron fields,**

**a wonderland of grace,**

**A beauty of nature,**

**a timeless place.**

**The harvest, a time of joy and pride,**

**The culmination of all the work inside.**

**For in the fields of saffron,**

**we find,**

**A world of wonder,**

**a world unconfined.**

**A beauty so rare,**

**a sight so grand,**

**A treasure of the earth,**

**a wonderland.**

**So let us cherish the saffron fields,**

**And all the beauty it kindly yields.**

**For in this land,**

**we find a trace,**

**Of nature's love,**

**of nature's grace.**

## CARRER

**In the journey of a career,**

**we find,**

**A beginning,**

**an end, a path to bind.**

**Money, love, degrees,**

**all in play,**

**A journey of discovery,**

**day by day.**

**The beginning,**

**a time of hope and fear,**

**A world of wonder,**

**yet to appear.**

**The path ahead,**

**a journey unknown,**

**A chance to grow,**

**a chance to be shown.**

**Degrees, a passport to a world of gain,**

**A chance to shine,**

**a chance to reign.**

Knowledge, a tool to reach new heights,

A key to unlock success, and all its sights.

But in the world of career and life,

There is more to gain, more to thrive.

Love, a companion to keep us sound,

A chance to share life's joys and bounds.

For in the end,

it is not just degrees,

Or money, or status,

or a life with ease.

It is the love we share,

the connections we find,

That truly make a career,

a life well defined.

So let us cherish the journey we're on,

And all the paths,

we've walked upon.

For in the end,

it is not just a career we find,

But a life well lived, a life one of a kind.

## MARKET

In the bustling market,

people roam,

A world of commerce,

a place called home.

Feelings run high,

as bargains are made,

A world of exchange,

a game well played.

But amidst the chaos and the noise,

**There is a sense of peace, a sense of poise.**

**As snow falls gently from the sky,**

**Love blooms in hearts,**

**as people pass by.**

**The market, a world of many tales,**

**Of triumphs and failures,**

**and all that entails.**

**But at its core,**

**it is a place of connection,**

**A place where hearts meet,**

**with no objection.**

**For in the market, as in life,**

**There is much to gain, much to strive.**

**But in the end,**

**it is the love we share,**

That truly makes life

a journey rare.

So let us cherish the market we know,

And all the feelings,

that come and go.

For in the end,

it is the love we show,

That truly makes life,

a beautiful snow.

## FROZEN RIVER

The river bed lies frozen,

cold and still,

A scene of winter,

a scene of chill.

Once a raging torrent,

**now a death bed,**

**Frozen in time,**

**with no life to be fed.**

**The icy grip,**

**of winter's nasty hold,**

**Has taken its toll,**

**on this river so bold.**

**Imagination runs wild,**

**in the icy wasteland,**

**A world of frost,**

**with no warmth at hand.**

**But as we stand in awe,**

**at the frozen river's side,**

**We can't help but feel,**

**a sense of apathy inside.**

**For though it is a wonder,**

**in its own right,**

**It is also a reminder,**

**of the bitter fight.**

**The fight for survival,**

**in a world so cold,**

**The fight for warmth,**

**in a story so old.**

**The frozen river,**

**a symbol of lifeless dread,**

**A reminder to us all,**

**to keep moving ahead.**

**For though the ice may hold us back,**

**And though the world may seem so black,**

**We must keep moving, with a heart so strong,**

And know that we will find,

where we truly belong.

CLOUDS AND THE SKY :

Above us is a canvas of blue,

A world of wonder,

a world so true.

The skies, a place of endless delight,

A place where dreams take flight.

The clouds,

hey dance and play,

A world of whimsy,

a world of display.

Snowflakes fall,

like diamonds from above,

world of magic,

a world of love.

The water droplets,

they float in the air,

A world of wonder,

a world so rare.

The skies and clouds,

a never-ending show,

A world of wonder,

a world that glows.

For in the skies,

we find our dreams,

A world of possibilities,

or so it seems.

A world of beauty,

a world of grace,

A world where we can find our rightful place.

So let us cherish the skies above,

And all the beauty,

that they so kindly serve.

For in the clouds and snowflakes,

we can see,

A world of wonder,

a world of possibility.

## LATE NIGHT CONVERSATIONS

Late night chat,

oh how it calls,

Whispers in the dark,

as time slowly falls.

A gentle hum,

a quiet sound,

**As we come together,**

**in the stillness around.**

**The world is quiet,**

**and so are we,**

**As we share our stories,**

**our hearts set free.**

**Words that flow,**

**like a river's song,**

**A conversation that can last all night long.**

**The glow of screens, the soft light,**

**As we connect in the quiet of the night.**

**There's no rush,**

**no need to go,**

**Just the peacefulness of this moment,**

**a chance to grow.**

**Late night chat,**

**oh how it brings,**

**A sense of comfort,**

**like a pair of wings.**

**Guiding us through the darkness of the night,**

**And leading us towards the morning light.**

**So let us embrace these moments,**

**dear,**

**And cherish the memories that we hold so near.**

**For in the quiet of the late night chat,**

**We find a place where we can simply be,**

**and that's where it's at.**

## DARK EYES

**In her dark eyes,**

**I see a world,**

**A place of naked feelings,**

**a love unfurled.**

**Her heart so open,**

**her soul so bare,**

**A loving girl,**

**beyond compare.**

**With every breath,**

**she loves so true,**

**A heart so pure,**

**it shines right through.**

**Her love is fierce,**

**her love is kind,**

**A love that knows no bounds,**

**no bind.**

**Yet sometimes, love can feel so cold,**

**A love that's loveless,**

**a love so old.**

**The pain it brings,**

**so deep inside,**

**A love that's lost,**

**a love that's died.**

**But still, this girl,**

**she holds on tight,**

**To hope and love,**

**in the darkest night.**

**For in her heart,**

**she knows it's true,**

**Love will find a way,**

**to see her through.**

**So let us learn from this loving girl,**

And cherish the love that's in our world.

For even in the darkest of days,

Love will shine its light, in so many ways.

## MUSINGS OF HEART

The heart is a mystery,

a wonder to behold,

A place of musings,

a story untold.

It beats with love,

and pumps with skill,

An energetic force,

that never stands still.

The feelings of the heart,

they run so deep,

A wellspring of emotions,

**that we often keep.**

**For in this beating organ,**

**lies a key,**

**To unlock the uniqueness,**

**of you and me.**

**The heart is a canvas,**

**painted with care,**

**A masterpiece of life,**

**that we all share.**

**It feels the pain,**

**and it feels the joy,**

**A symphony of emotions,**

**that we can't destroy.**

**So let your heart feel,**

**and let it soar,**

Let it beat with love,

forevermore.

For in this beating organ,

lies a gift,

A chance to live life, and all its lift.

## WETLAND

In the midst of nature,

lies a land so wet,

Where grooves and grasslands,

meet and beget.

A wetland so lush,

with life abound,

A place of imagination,

where beauty is found.

The grooves and the grass,

**they dance in the breeze,**

**A symphony of nature,**

**that never will freeze.**

**And in this wetland,**

**we see a courtesy,**

**A balance of life,**

**that's so full of diversity.**

**From the smallest of creatures,**

**to the tallest of trees,**

**This wetland is home,**

**to so many beings.**

**And though it may seem,**

**like a place so remote,**

**It's a vital ecosystem,**

**that we must devote.**

**For the wetland is a gem,**

**in our natural world,**

**A precious resource,**

**that's often unfurled.**

**And with courtesy and care,**

**we must protect,**

**This wetland of life, that we cannot neglect.**

## LIFELESSNESS

**Lifeless and empty,**
**The world seems without meaning.**
**But look beyond the surface,**
**And a mesmerizing beauty lies gleaming.**

**Nature's wonders, so vast and grand,**
**Nurture and sustain, with a gentle hand.**
**From the depths of the ocean,**
**To the soaring heights of the land.**

**In the midst of our miseries,**
**Let us seek solace in the natural world.**
**For there we can find respite,**

And our souls can be unfurled.

So let us embrace the beauty around us,
And find meaning in the cycle of life.
For amidst our sorrows and our struggles,
Nature offers us a respite from our strife.

## Endless race

In the midst of life's endless race,

We often forget to stop and embrace,

The beauty of nature,

the wonder of life,

And all the struggles and strife.

But in the depths of our hearts,

There lies a love that never departs,

A sympathy for all that is lifeless,

And a yearning for beauty that is boundless.

For even in the darkest of times,

We can find solace in nature's rhymes,

**A gentle reminder that we are not alone,**

**And that even lifeless things can be shown.**

**And though some may scorn and deride,**

**The beauty of nature cannot be denied,**

**For in its midst,**

**we find a sense of peace,**

**And a love that never seems to cease.**

**So let us take a moment each day,**

**To appreciate nature in our own special way,**

**To feel the sympathy that lies within,**

**And to embrace the beauty that we've been given.**

**Book Title: Verses of Life: A Collection of Poems**

**Summary:**

**"Verses of Life" is a collection of poems that reflects the author's personal experiences, thoughts, and emotions. The poems capture various moments in life and offer insight, inspiration, and comfort to readers. From love and loss to hope**

**and perseverance, the poems explore a range of human emotions and experiences. The collection is a heartfelt and honest reflection on life's journey, with each poem offering a unique perspective and message.**

**Table of Contents:**

**Each section of the book contains a collection of poems related to the theme of that section. The poems are written in a variety of styles and structures, from free verse to sonnets. Through the use of vivid imagery, powerful language, and evocative metaphors, the author invites readers to join them on a journey of self-discovery, growth, and understanding.**

**"Verses of Life" is a moving and insightful collection that speaks to the human experience in a profound and meaningful way. Whether read from cover to cover or opened at random, the poems in this collection are sure to resonate with readers and offer comfort, wisdom, and inspiration on life's journey.**

# Contents

9 798889 861843

Printed by Libri Plureos GmbH in Hamburg, Germany